Sener Saltürk

Matilda's World and the Real One

About Roald Dahl´s "Matilda"

GRIN Verlag

Bibliografische Information der Deutschen Nationalbibliothek:

Die Deutsche Bibliothek verzeichnet diese Publikation in der Deutschen National-
bibliografie; detaillierte bibliografische Daten sind im Internet über http://dnb.d-
nb.de/ abrufbar.

Imprint:

Copyright © 2005 GRIN Verlag GmbH
Druck und Bindung: Books on Demand GmbH, Norderstedt Germany
ISBN: 978-3-656-30388-6

This book at GRIN:

http://www.grin.com/en/e-book/204005/matilda-s-world-and-the-real-one

Matilda's World and the Real One

I. Introduction

Taken for granted that children around, say, 10 years old *do* have an idea of what kind of a world they are living in by considering the world's immediate, esp. social, impact on them (school, parents, friends, neighbourhood, teachers etc.), it goes almost without saying that they have to make use of their own fantasy in order to produce secondary worlds which become a necessity. The term *world* can point to a number of directions but what we can state about it is that children – *because* they have a somewhat narrow scope – have a better access to fictional worlds that are, of course, also to be found in any fairy tale, thus in any children's book from Huckleberry Finn to Harry Potter. The world*s* which are portrayed in these offer an ersatz world, one that seems more adventurous and fascinating to any child, regardless of how they consider their own reality to be. The reason for this is the reality they are born into, a reality that has to do with any sort of dangers which cause a constant threat to them.

The real world does not satisfy all of their needs and, above all, they do not rule (in) it. Their scope of action is quite restricted due to their little age, experience and – a circumstance quite clearly dealt with in Matilda – their bodies.

Though children's books not infrequently take on the subject of children suffering under their own weaknesses, the major difference between the world in these books and the real world is that in the latter they cannot define the rules, nor *can* they rule. In a fictional world, however, they can become heroes and masters of their own fate, or even, anything and anyone. Here children can become free in an existential sense of the word. In order to gain this freedom the child must cope with a number of different and quite difficult and dangerous tasks. But what sort of world is it actually? An aforementioned ersatz world, a parallel world or just a copy of the real world they are desperately striving to escape from?

In any case, these fictitious worlds do not only include the "things in it" but quite frequently (cf. Harry Potter, Huck Finn etc.), focus strongly on their protagonists, a fictional child that is in many ways *like* any other child save in one thing: he or she is capable of 'doing things' the others cannot, thus being enabled to change the status quo of things (or of the world). This status quo, i.e. conflicts children generally encounter, is depicted in ironic, quite often exaggerated ways that the child heroes have to face and overcome. Of course, in order to accomplish this, it takes an extraordinary child and it is no coincidence that many a 'successful' children's book either carries its protagonist(s)'s name in the title or is actually named after them. As is Roald Dahl's Matilda.

As for the world Matilda lives in, it contains many elements of different genres (such as fairy tales etc.) that I will pay my closer attention to, hoping to yield some information on what these worlds include and what makes them so attractive to children and approach to the fantasies and the fantasy world of children.

II. Matilda universe: what/who is real, what/who is fiction?

As the writer and critic A.S. Byatt points out in her review on Harry Potter, children books contain *caricatures* of the real world which "has trains, hospitals, newspapers and competitive sport[1]." So does 'Matilda'. She gets her beloved books by Dickens, Austen, Kipling, Orwell etc. from Mrs Phelps, the librarian at the 'local' library, in order to devour them on the spot or at home. As for 'local', we are not told by the narrator in which particular town the narration takes place. Thanks to some characters' names such as Mrs Wormwood's and Mrs Phelps' we can suppose that the characters in Matilda are living in an English speaking country, and anyway, does the author really tell us that it is not a nice little village somewhere in Australia and what actually, except the (British English) language that is used, could make us think otherwise? Spain is mentioned at the end of the novel (p. 236) which can be reached from, say, New Zealand as well!). Coincidence? It seems simply unimportant since the locations and the different characters (which are anything but insipid!) act as variables in a parable story, actually not very much different from the one Matilda herself is reading at the beginning of the story: Orwell's 'Animal Farm.' Just as each character in Animal Farm stands for either iconic personalities (Stalin, Lenin, Hitler, Goebbles) and/or for human vices and virtues (horses and donkeys = efficiency, loyalty; dogs and pigs = malice, intelligence), the characters in Matilda stand for universal human characteristics. In many ways, even the characters themselves are 'caricatures' of real people. Or are there really personalities *that* superficial such as Matilda's parents, Mr and Mrs Wormwood, in real life, not to mention, of course, Matilda's superhuman powers or Fred's speaking parrot that says: "Rattle my bones? (p. 43)? Or "The Trunchbull"? Certainly not. But there are people in real life who are *like* them, sharing many of their features, esp. in terms of morals, thus their connection to and (lack of) sensitivity for both power and justice. And therefore the characters, and to some extent even Matilda's character (which I must sadly admit), are mere caricatures, since they are sketched in an exaggerated way, being reduced to only some characteristics (Matilda = amiable, nice, [very] intelligent, morally aware); Mr Wormwood = ugly (even "ratty", p. 23), unscrupulous, preferring money to (loving) his children; Mrs Wormwood = extremely superficial, uneducated, slovenly etc. But even these characters do not necessarily have to be perceived as disagreeable as one might expect since they have a comical, ridiculous side to them which distinguishes them from "real" villains. And what is more: nobody gets killed

---

[1] Source: http://www.theage.com.au/articles/2003/07/18/1058035189828.html?oneclick=true

(except for Miss Honey's father but this happened in the past) – after all, this is a children's book.

Of course this has nothing to do with any sort of weakness in Dahl's ability to portray characters, quite the contrary. It is these dualisms such as good and evil, or, to be more accurate, good versus evil, which constitute the story's moral. There must be villains so as to render Matilda (even more) amiable: Matilda's real antagonist is, of course, Mrs Trunchbull, the dreaded and ("really") villainous headmistress. That's because, in contrast to Matilda's parents, she *embodies* malice and, what is more, there is hardly anything about her that could make children laugh at her. Despite her outward appearance, she is definitely *not* ridiculous.

She is the greatest threat even to adult readers who compassionately live through the poor children's fears of Miss Trunchbull. But Matilda's mere presence and the instant identification of the reader with her render even Miss Trunchbull "vincible" all the same.

The revelation of such exaggerated a character like Miss Trunchbull emphasizes the above mentioned dualism. It focuses on only some *distinctive* features or characteristics which is a technique frequently employed in caricatures. Any information that might distract the reader's attention from this, is redundant and will destroy the caricature (note that ca*ri*cature contains the originally Latin word "*ri*dere" = to laugh).

Miss Honey's is probably the only amiable adult in the entire book. Her character, as Matilda's, is diametrically opposed to that of Miss Trunchbull. She is sensitive, caring and *reasonable*, in contrast to the other adults in the story (except for Miss Phelps, the librarian!).

And, of course, it would be useless trying to find fault with her because there is none (no cynicism intended). Except maybe that she is too honest, too kind, too dear. And it would likewise have been absurd had Dahl portrayed her vices as well. Because this is *not* the real world, which has so few heroes (except icons, maybe, such as that of Ché Guevara – who I personally consider anything but a hero), where even an act of good will might result in a disaster. The world of a fairy tale must not have ambiguity. That is why we are only provided with information which is relevant for the sake of the fictional narration a story that takes place in another *world*, that of the fantasies of (both) children (and adults).

III. Themes/Conflicts: "My parents are aliens"

Notwithstanding the unique way Dahl reveals his characters and the story, he makes use of the most prominent themes and conflicts that are well comparable to those in many modern children's books[2] (his individual artistic contribution is, of course, beyond dispute). The main conflicts which are prevailing throughout the entire novel are "my parents are aliens", "my teacher is a hero/demon", "injustice", esp. (but not exceptionally) done to children.

In real life only one of these conflicts would be simply unbearable for any child which he/she could never manage to cope with. In Matilda, however, *all* of them occur and hit the life of the five (!) year-old Matilda simultaneously! Whatever the horrors of real life that some of our little ones have to go through, the conflicts in Matilda do more or less nothing but *resemble* them, "only" extremely exaggeratedly.

Take, for instance, the "my parents are aliens"-topic.

There is a father who does not care at bit about his two children although he shows some "affection" for his son Michael, Matilda's (not too bright) elder brother, and a mother who wishes nothing more than Matilda be married to a rich man (or someone who has only money in his mind, such as her husband).

As for her father's affection to Michael, it is just because he feels he must provide his son with crafty knowledge about how to "diddle" (p. 23) people:

"'But I don't mind telling young Mike here about it seeing he'll be joining me in the [car dealing] business one day.' Ignoring Matilda, he turned to his son and said, 'I am always glad to buy a car when some fool has been crashing the gears so badly they're worn out and rattle like mad. I get it cheap. Then all I do is mix a lot of sawdust with the oil in the gear-box and it runs as sweet as a nut.'" (p. 23).

The mother, indulging in her vanity and superficiality, approves fully to her husband's ways of raising their children. *These* parents are actually only fond of their own children when they are not around, otherwise they are simply disturbing while they are watching TV (which they do all the time):

"Mummy," Matilda said, "would you mind if I ate my supper in the dining-room so I could read my book?"

The father glanced up sharply. "*I* would mind!" he snapped. "Supper is a family gathering and no one leaves the table till it's over!"

---

[2] Wikipedia: Children's Books

"But we're not at the table," Matilda said. "We never are. We're always eating off our knees and watching the telly."

"What's wrong with watching the telly, may I ask?" the father said. (p. 28).

Of course, the *world* Dahl portrays is quite odd and in the example mentioned above he employs a great deal of irony by providing us with a (supposedly) daily living-room scene of a family, only the behaviour of both parents and Matilda are right the opposite of what one would expect. But what is most important about this scene is the fact that Matilda has not only bad parents but she has actually *none*: Mentally she is an orphan, a famous topic of children's books, of course. And, what is more, this conflict has to be solved somehow during the course of the novel!

And there is yet another famous topic that emerges in this scene: the sense of justice and injustice. The parents have no sense of morals but Matilda does:

"Can you really turn the mileage back with an electric drill?" young Michael asked.

"I'm telling you trade secrets," the father said. "So don't you go talking about this to anyone else. You don't want me put in jug, do you?"

"I won't tell a soul," the boy said. "Do you do this to many yars, dad?" […]

Matilda, who had been listening closely, said, "But daddy, that's even more dishonest than the sawdust. It's disgusting. You're cheating people who trust you."

"If you don't like it then don't eat the food in this house," the father said. "It's bought with the profits."

"It's dirty money," Matilda said. "I hate it." […]

"Who the heck do you think you are," he shouted, "The Archbishop of Canterbury or something, preaching to me about honesty?"

Young Michael, who is only a little older than Matilda, is an example representing a child who is already being "cheated" by his parents, especially by the father. There is no objection on his side to their parents' machinations. There is, by the way, hardly any information as to what Mrs. Wormwood's attitude is towards her son (as is about Michael and Matilda). Mrs. Wormwood and her husband get on astonishingly well – to them, Matilda is the one who 'causes problems.' And it might come to some readers' minds why the parents actually "keep" Matilda. Each one of them has a reason for rejecting her. The father rejects her because she cannot be of any help in his (cheating) car business – probably because she is a girl. The mother who is obviously in charge of raising her daughter tells her teacher, Miss

Honey (who has noticed Matilda's astounding talents and intelligence) trying to explain the ignorant parents that their child is a prodigy:

"A girl should think about making herself look attractive so she can get a good husband later on. Looks is more important than books, Miss Hunky…"

"The name is Honey," Miss Honey said. (p. 97)

So what do they actually teach her, a girl of only five years? Well, actually nothing else than to 'shut up [father] and marry some rich bloke one day [mother].'

These quotations illustrate in an unusually clear way the family union of the Wormwoods. They are (again) weird, exceptional, crazy and, considering what a child really needs, "Dahlishly" devilish.

But when we have a closer look to what happens in this family, we realize that the Wormwoods are not that exceptional because there are a number of Wormwoods in reality. Not seldom reality looks somewhat like this: parents are usually "stressed out" and do not have to *tell* their kids to watch the "telly" (nor *not* to do so) because they do it anyway, nor even ask about how school was etc. And who says that many a father does not raise his son in a typically manlike way, thus not paying attention to what *he* would like to do or become one day and instead just pushing him into some "business" of his own, e.g. by simply overstraining him by means of a daily "soft terror" because he wants him to become a professional soccer football player? After all, once Mr Wormwood is gone, he is not going to pass any kingship to his son but a garage that is not a customer-friendly one and not every mother is an angel either.

It is, above all, moral values that are passed on the children which are important. The child reader, of course, is made more sensitive of what 'is right and wrong' and sides with Miss Honey and Matilda.

My teacher is a hero/demon

The action in Matilda takes place to a large extent at school where she encounters two so fundamentally different (adult) characters, Miss Honey and Miss Trunchbull. Whether Miss Honey is really a "hero" or not, is hard to say because on the one hand she is a child-loving, even angel-like character and a first-rate pedagogue, but on the other hand she, towards the end of the book – when her own (past) life is unfolded –, turns out to have once been a victim of Miss Trunchbull's. The latter, however, is undoubtedly a demon since she is furnished with every sort of maliciousness that might 'guarantee' any child permanent nightmares. Even so, Miss Honey and Miss Trunchbull must be seen clearly as antagonists – at least from a children's view they are.

Injustice

The greatest injustice Matilda and all the children of the school have to experience comes from the headmistress, Miss Trunchbull. In fact, all of her actions, both at school *and* in her private life – as we come to know in the fifth last chapter of the book entitled "Miss Honey's Story" (p. 193-205) – are themed malice or injustice.

Again, it is irony and a great deal of exaggeration (hence "caricatures") that Dahl employs here to characterize Miss Trunchbull. Her actions, among others, include her refusal of Miss Honey's initiative to let Matilda sit in the senior class: "So she has learnt a few tables by heart, has she?" Miss Trunchbull barked. "My dear woman, that doesn't make her a genius! It makes her a parrot!" (p. 87). She doesn't allow one of the girls called Amanda to wear pigtails ("Chop 'em off and throw 'em in the dustbin, you understand?", p. 114) and hurls (!) her through the playground, "spinning round and round, and soon Amanda Thripp was travelling so fast she became a blur, and suddenly, with a mighty grunt, the Trunchbull let go of the pigtails and Amanda went sailing like a rocket right over the wire fence of the playground and high up into the sky." (p. 115).

Another victim who experiences injustice is Bruce Bogtrotter who Miss Trunchbull picks up and punishes in front of the entire school children by forcing him to eat an enormous cake for having (allegedly) stolen Miss Trunchbull's cake: "Don't lie to me, Bogtrotter!" barked the Trunchbull. "The cook saw you! What's more, she saw you eating it!" (p. 121). During another incident she grabs Rupert by the hair (and later also by the *ear*) and whirls him around in the air because he fails in correctly answering Miss Trunchbull's math "interrogation" (p. 150) etc.

The revelation of (injustice committed by) Miss Trunchbull is explained in every little detail and roughly half of the novel is dedicated to the "Miss Trunchbull issue". For this reason her actions are much more important than the ones of Matilda's parents, indeed, the novel would hardly work without her. Unlike Mr and Mrs Wormwood, Miss Trunchbull is a real horror to children, especially because she is the only one who harms them both mentally and *physically*. Another difference between Matilda's parents and her is that she represents a tyrant and a demon which is even worse than every child's nightmare of having parents who do not care about them.

The theme injustice is closely connected with that of moral. Both the crafty Mr Wormwood and The Trunchbull represent amoral behaviour which they express by means of their greed, in which The Trunchbull is far more brutal and malicious than him. There is, however, a striking similarity between them: both fail to fulfil the minimum requirements of their duty to children and do exactly the opposite of what they are required to do: as parents, Mr and Mrs Wormwood pay no attention to their children at all instead of loving (or at least caring for) them. The Trunchbull punishes the pupils rather than educating them. Matilda is, as the reader is, perfectly aware of this injustice bestowed upon her and understands fully what is right and wrong. After this she takes action on disposing of them once and for all. Of course, it is not in a five year old girl's power to tackle problems like these. *Only* in a fiction story and *only* a girl that is as supernaturally gifted like Matilda can overcome such miseries that in our reality would ruin both character and life of any child.

Injustice, it seems, is not that quite uncommon in a child's life. While in Matilda highly unusual problems are approached in a likewise unusual manner (by an unusual child such as Matilda), in reality only a fraction of these would tear children apart.

Overcoming Injustice (done to oneself or to others)

From the outset, i.e. after the reader has gathered enough antipathy toward Matilda's father, Matilda launches her counterattack which is even at that point not merely her own fight against their parents but also some sort of revenge for the "diddling" business of her father, thus she takes revenge both for herself *and* all the other poor victims, i.e. customers, of her father's.

The Superglue episode (p. 30-37) clearly indicates that this girl is not going to let a matter rest. The next episode (The Ghost) is a continuation of Matilda's 'little' revenge on her parents. And it is in these chapters of the novel that Matilda foreshadows what else she will be capable of during the course of the novel. While her parents seem to be easily cheated, as in the 'parrot' episode, Miss Trunchbull, does not seem all that easy to tackle. At the end of the novel, of course, she beats The Trunchbull scathingly and rids the other poor children from her. At the same time she makes sure that justice is done to Miss Honey as well, by unusual means, of course.

But we must ask ourselves whether Matilda necessarily has to be equipped with supernatural powers and to what extent the story would make sense without these. One explanation to this question is obviously that children in general love reading fantasy stories and that many a child hero does have such powers such as Harry Potter etc. Another explanation is that the problems they are charged with would otherwise be much more difficult to approach. And how do you want to beat The Trunchbull who embodies a child nightmare if not by these means? The problems seem to be simply impossible to tackle *without* them. This, I think, shows that "in reality" children have hardly any powers at their disposal to change anything about their situation but are totally dependent on the adults who impose their will on them.

The main reason for this is, again, moral. Moral can be used by anyone to justify their actions, and for almost any action one can make use (or better *ab*use) of moral. Although children as a rule know what is right and what is wrong, against adults, however, who are more experienced in any matter (and thus "equipped" with means of manipulation), they are powerless. Everyone has his or her own justifications for their actions, as even Mr (and Mrs) Wormwood and Miss Trunchbull have, no matter how unmoral they might seem. The advantages adults have are above all linguistic and knowledge-related. Especially the Trunchbull makes explicit use of these so as to achieve her foul ends, i.e. to intimidate the children. It seems, actually, that Miss Trunchbull simply wishes that there were no children or at least that they would absolutely behave themselves according to how *she* thinks they ought to behave so she would not have to bother about them – which is again something she has in common with Mr and Mrs Wormwood. The ultimate irony about Miss Trunchbull is that she has the wrong job – she is more a gaoler than a headmistress or teacher:

"You ignorant little slug!" the Trunchbull bellowed. "You witless weed! You empty-headed hamster! You stupid glob of glue!" (p. 148) etc.

Rescue of the Princess

As mentioned above, Matilda is not selfish in her actions but acts also for the sake of others. She possesses a sense of justice which includes all people, e.g. she sympathises with her father's "diddled" customers because they are cheated etc. But what is more – as she discovers at the very end of the novel – she gets *angry* if she is confronted with sheer injustice. She seems as she were *allergic* to injustice. And I think that this characteristic of hers renders her a most amiable child. She cannot stand injustice. In some sense she resembles a well-armed angel sent by (an angry) god to fight the devils which surround her. Her power ceases when she does not feel angry anymore, obviously because there is no need to tackle something: "This morning," Matilda said, "just for fun I tried to push something over with my eyes and I couldn't do it. Nothing moved. I didn't even feel the hotness building up behind my eyeballs. The power had gone. I think I've lost it completely."

The ultimate aim in doing this is, of course, to let justice prevail. And there is another character whose life has been so unjustly determined by the malicious Miss Trunchbull – Miss Honey.

The "rescue" of Miss Honey is comparable to that of a princess, a topic which has been widely written about in literature. Miss Honey is very much like a princess, sharing many characteristics with one. First of all she is not only as a teacher a perfectly warm-hearted person who cares about her pupils. She is deeply concerned about Matilda and is the only one who notices both Matilda's talent and supernatural powers. In fact, she is the only person who knows this secret of Matilda's. Another reason for Miss Honey's resembling a princess is that is always well-meaning, even towards her aunt, Miss Trunchbull:

"'Mrs D, Mrs I, Mrs FFI

Mrs C, Mrs U, Mrs LTY.

That spells difficulty.'

'How perfectly ridiculous!" snorted the Trunchbull. Why are all these women married? And anyway you're not meant to teach poetry when you're teaching spelling. Cut it out in future, Miss Honey.'

'But it does teach them some of the harder words wonderfully well,' Miss Honey murmured."

Due to her restricted power as a teacher Miss Honey cannot "cut out" the persistent injustice of Miss Trunchbull. Even so, she tries to be as friendly as she always is. There is but one problem about Miss Honey's behaviour: even though she is trying to teach her pupils to the best of her abilities, she cannot avert the constant danger of Miss Trunchbull's presence where anything can happen (and which does happen!). This renders Miss Honey a victim – she is *not* a hero. Only with Matilda's help which is of course supernatural does she overcome the Trunchbull. This means that in real life Miss Honey would have remained a victim just as her unprotected pupils! She too needs to be rescued:

"'It's writing something!' screamed Nigel. 'The chalk is writing something!'

And indeed it was." (p. 220) […]

'Give my Jenny her wages

Give my Jenny the house

Then get out of here.

If you don't, I will come

And get you

I will come and get you

I will come and get you

Like you got me.

I am watching you

Agatha.'" (p. 223)

This is Miss Trunchbull's (=Agatha's) last appearance in the novel. 'Jenny' is Miss Honey's first name. Matilda "makes" Miss Honey's dead father write his message to Miss Trunchbull on the blackboard. Finally, everything turns out alright. While all of a sudden Mr and Mrs have to flee the country due to Mr Wormwood's illegal dealings –Matilda's last encounter with her parents takes roughly two to three minutes – they do not care about Matilda (of course) which causes a circumstance to solve the "orphan" problem: Miss becoming Matilda's new mother. The more or less total absence of sexuality in the novel or any notion of it seems rather peculiar. There is no mentioning of a boyfriend of Miss Honey, not even any talk about a former partnership with somebody. Of course Miss Honey (who is twenty-three, by the way) has no opportunity to talk about these subjects to Matilda and the novel is not about such matters. But regarding the "princess" idea, I would say, Miss Honey is not devoted to any man but to children. Miss Honey who is the embodiment of warmth and goodness, of heart, must not have a partner – this, I dare say, would spoil the idea of her "innocence".

I think, it is essential to stress the idea of reading Matilda as a parabola and to compare it with the effects to which the occasions described in the novel correspond. What if Matilda had no powers at all, a bright girl whose talents would always remain unnoticed, if Miss Honey were well-meaning but always condescended, if Miss Trunchbull would go on tormenting everybody while Mr Wormwood would put saw-dust into the gearbox, Mrs Wormwood "munching on her meal with her eyes glued to the American soap-opera on the screen," (p. 27)? The answer is: We would then get a perfect example of the reality of many a Matilda from our, that is, *non*-fictional world.